SandCastle 2

Opposites

New and Old

Kelly Doudna

ABDO
Publishing Company

Published by SandCastle™, an imprint of ABDO Publishing Company, 4940 Viking Drive, Edina, Minnesota 55435.

Printed in the United States.

Photo credits: Comstock, Corel, Definitive Stock, Digital Stock, DigitalVision, John Deere, PhotoDisc.

Library of Congress Cataloging-in-Publication Data

Doudna, Kelly, 1963-
    New and old / Kelly Doudna.
      p. cm. -- (Opposites)
    Summary: Simple rhymes point out the differences between new and old.
    ISBN 1-57765-148-0 (alk. paper) -- ISBN 1-57765-282-7 (set)
     1. English language--Synonyms and antonyms--Juvenile literature. 2. Readers (Primary) [1. Readers. 2. English language--Synonyms and antonyms.] I. Title.

PE1591 .D65 2000
428.1--dc21

99-046487

The SandCastle concept, content, and reading method have been reviewed and approved by a national advisory board including literacy specialists, librarians, elementary school teachers, early childhood education professionals, and parents.

Let Us Know

After reading the book, SandCastle would like you to tell us your stories about reading. What is your favorite page? Was there something hard that you needed help with? Share the ups and downs of learning to read. We want to hear from you! To get posted on the Abdo Publishing Company Web site, send us email at:

sandcastle@abdopub.com

About SandCastle™

Nonfiction books for the beginning reader

- Basic concepts of phonics are incorporated with integrated language methods of reading instruction. Most words are short, and phrases, letter sounds, and word sounds are repeated.

- Readability is determined by the number of words in each sentence, the number of characters in each word, and word lists based on curriculum frameworks.

- Full-color photography reinforces word meanings and concepts.

- "Words I Can Read" list at the end of each book teaches basic elements of grammar, helps the reader recognize the words in the text, and builds vocabulary.

- Reading levels are indicated by the number of flags on the castle.

Look for more SandCastle books
in these three reading levels:

Level 1 (one flag)	**Level 2** (two flags)	**Level 3** (three flags)

Grades Pre-K to K 5 or fewer words per page	**Grades K to 1** 5 to 10 words per page	**Grades 1 to 2** 10 to 15 words per page

This teddy bear is worn.

It is **old**.

My teddy bear is **new**.

It is fun to hold.

This wagon is **old**.

It used to carry hay.

This mower is **new**.

It cuts grass all day.

This house is **old**.

It fell down.

Our house is **new**.

We live in town.

My grandpa is **old**.

His head is almost bare.

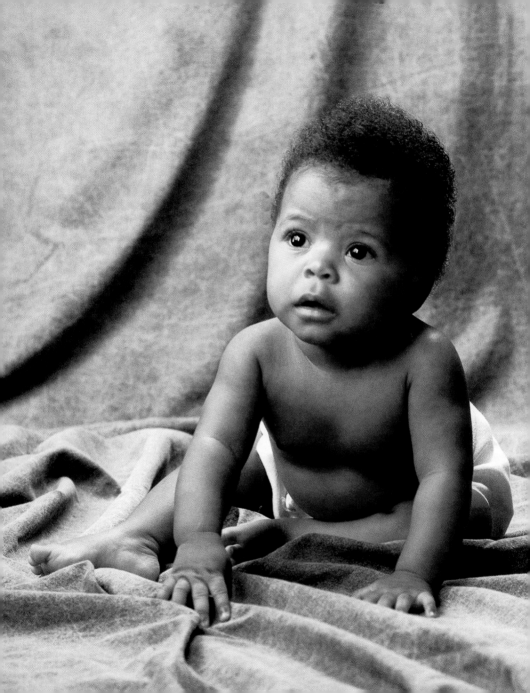

A baby is **new**.

It needs much care.

What do you see that is **new** or **old**?

Words I Can Read

Nouns

A noun is a person, place, or thing

baby (BAY-bee) p. 19
care (KAIR) p. 19
day (DAY) p. 11
grandpa (GRAND-pah) p. 17
grass (GRASS) p. 11
hay (HAY) p. 9
head (HED) p. 17
house (HOWSS) pp. 13, 15
mower (MOH-uhr) p. 11
teddy bear (TED-ee bair) pp. 5, 7
town (TOWN) p. 15
wagon (WAG-uhn) p. 9

Verbs

A verb is an action or being word

carry (KA-ree) p. 9
cuts (KUHTSS) p. 11
do (DOO) p. 21

fell (FEL) p. 13
hold (HOHLD) p. 7
is (IZ) pp. 5, 7, 9, 11, 13, 15, 17, 19, 21
live (LIV) p. 15
needs (NEEDZ) p. 19
see (SEE) p. 21
used (YOOZD) p. 9

Adjectives

An adjective describes something

bare (BAIR) p. 17
fun (FUHN) p. 7
his (HIZ) p. 17
much (MUHCH) p. 19
my (MYE) pp. 7, 17
new (NOO) pp. 7, 11, 15, 19, 21
old (OHLD) pp. 5, 9, 13, 17, 21
our (AR) p. 15
this (THISS) pp. 5, 9, 11, 13
worn (WORN) p. 5

Picture Words

hay

teddy bear

mower

wagon

Word Families

Words that have the same vowel
and ending letters

-old	-own
hold	down
old	town

-ay	-are
day	bare
hay	care

24